Original title:
Crafting the Core of Closeness

Copyright © 2024 Swan Charm
All rights reserved.

Author: Sara Säde
ISBN HARDBACK: 978-9916-86-737-2
ISBN PAPERBACK: 978-9916-86-738-9
ISBN EBOOK: 978-9916-86-739-6

The Art of Being Near

In quiet moments, hearts align,
Soft whispers weave a gentle sign.
Distance fades when souls connect,
The art of being near, perfect.

In the Hush of Togetherness

When silence speaks in tender ways,
Comfort lingers, softly stays.
In the hush, our spirits blend,
Togetherness, a cherished friend.

Layers of Love Unfolded

With every glance, a story told,
Layers of love, both shy and bold.
Petals bloom in gentle light,
Unfolding hearts, a sweet delight.

The Glow of Familiarity

In every laugh, a spark ignites,
Familiar faces, warm delights.
A glow that radiates from within,
Comfort found where love begins.

Bound by Light

In shadows deep where secrets lie,
The whispers of the stars comply.
A beacon glows, a path ignites,
Together we shall chase the nights.

Across the tides, we drift as one,
Each heartbeat forged, our journey spun.
With every pulse, the cosmos sings,
Forever bound by what love brings.

Through storms and still, our spirits soar,
Hand in hand, we seek for more.
The skies illuminate our way,
In unity, we find our day.

The light of dawn, it breaks anew,
In every hue, I see your view.
With every breath, our promise tight,
We are forever bound by light.

The Heart's Canvas

Upon the canvas, colors blend,
A tapestry where dreams transcend.
With strokes of passion, bold and bright,
Each whisper paints the endless night.

Emotions flow like rivers wide,
In every hue, our truths abide.
Together crafting what we feel,
The art of love, its power real.

With gentle hands, we shape our fate,
Each masterpiece, we celebrate.
In tones of warmth, our spirits rise,
A gallery beneath the skies.

In every shade, our stories flow,
An endless dance, a vibrant glow.
My heart, your canvas, intertwined,
A work of art, by love defined.

Intertwining Destinies

Fates that twine like vines at dusk,
In every glance, a sacred trust.
Paths collide, a dance divine,
In every step, our souls align.

With whispers soft, we forge our way,
Through winding trails where shadows play.
Together facing night and day,
In love's embrace, we choose to stay.

Through trials faced, we grow in grace,
In shared moments, we find our place.
Our destinies, like stars, will weave,
In unity, we shall believe.

Hand in hand, we shift the tides,
In every heart, our depth resides.
A journey mapped by fate's design,
Intertwined, your soul in mine.

Found in Togetherness

In laughter shared and silent sighs,
A bond that strengthens, never dies.
Through storms we walk, in sunshine bask,
In every moment, love's the task.

The warmth of hands, a gentle touch,
In shared glances, we mean so much.
Together on this winding road,
In every heartbeat, a shared code.

With dreams aligned, we dare to fly,
Beneath the vast and open sky.
In unity, we find our song,
A melody where we belong.

Through ups and downs, we rise anew,
In every challenge, we push through.
Together forged, forever blessed,
In togetherness, we find our rest.

The Silence Between Us

In quiet moments, whispers fade,
Where shadows linger, softly laid.
A gaze unbroken, hearts entwine,
In silence deep, our souls align.

The world outside feels far away,
In breaths we share, the night turns gray.
Yet in this hush, a bond is found,
In tranquil space, love's purest sound.

With every heartbeat, time stands still,
A tender peace, a sacred thrill.
These gentle pauses, shared embrace,
In silence, we find our hidden place.

The moonlight shimmers, casting dreams,
In quietude, we trace the seams.
Of stories woven, a soft caress,
In stillness profound, our hearts confess.

So let the world spin fast and free,
Within this space, it's you and me.
In whispered truths, let love renew,
In silence shared, we find what's true.

Embrace of Dreams United

In the twilight's soft embrace,
We drift through realms, a sacred space.
With every heartbeat, dreams align,
Together, lost in the divine.

A tapestry of starlit skies,
In whispered hopes, love never dies.
With open hearts, we take the flight,
Through boundless dreams, we chase the light.

Hand in hand, we weave the night,
In shadows deep, our spirits bright.
With every wish, a promise made,
In dreams united, we won't fade.

The dawn emergent, golden rays,
Reflect the love in myriad ways.
Together, we shall rise and soar,
In dreams entwined, forevermore.

Through every storm, we find the calm,
In our embrace, a healing balm.
With laughter shared and hearts so bold,
In dreams' embrace, true tales unfold.

Echoes of a Gentle Touch

In twilight's glow, your fingers trace,
Through dusk's embrace, we find our pace.
With gentle strokes, our stories blend,
In every touch, a timeless mend.

The softest whispers fill the air,
In every heartbeat, love laid bare.
Through silence shared, our spirits soar,
In echoes sweet, we crave for more.

Each brush of skin, a spark ignites,
In tender moments, lost in flights.
With every caress, the world refrains,
In gentle echoes, love remains.

The night unfolds with dreams so sweet,
Your gentle touch, my heart's retreat.
With every sigh, a rhythm flows,
In echoes soft, our passion glows.

Through every dawn that breaks anew,
In every touch, I find the true.
Together, hand in hand we'll stand,
In echoes deep, our love's command.

Mosaic of Shared Moments

In a garden of laughter, we bloom,
Petals of joy break through the gloom.
Whispers of sunlight on our face,
Every glance a sacred place.

Stitching memories, thread by thread,
In every silence, words unsaid.
Moments flash like fireflies' flight,
Guiding us through the velvet night.

Underneath the stars, hearts align,
Every beat, a pulse divine.
Footsteps mark the path we've made,
In this dance, fears start to fade.

We paint our dreams on canvas wide,
Each stroke a story, side by side.
Colors blend in perfect harmony,
In this art, we find our glee.

As seasons shift and time moves on,
In our hearts, the bond stays strong.
The mosaic shines, a vibrant hue,
Forever blessed, just me and you.

Echoes of Intimacy

In soft-lit rooms where secrets dwell,
Whispers weave a tender spell.
Each sigh a note in our sweet song,
Echoes of love where we belong.

Eyes meet like bridges over streams,
Connecting us in shared dreams.
Laughter dances in the air,
A gentle pulse of hearts laid bare.

Fingers trace familiar lines,
Mapping out our heartfelt signs.
Every touch, a spark ignites,
Guiding us through the quiet nights.

In stolen glances, truth reveals,
A deeper bond that love conceals.
In the silence, we find our voice,
Echoes of love, the heart's true choice.

Together we create our space,
In this intimacy, we find grace.
Wrapped in warmth, the world fades away,
In our echoes, forever we'll stay.

Weaving Warmth in Silence

In the hush of night, we reside,
A tapestry woven, side by side.
Threads of warmth in every pause,
Comfort found without a cause.

Softly spoken dreams unfold,
In quiet moments, love's pure gold.
Every heartbeat, a silent tune,
Beneath the watchful silver moon.

Hands entwined, no need for words,
In this stillness, our hearts are heard.
Understanding flows like gentle streams,
Crafting life from fragile dreams.

We share the weight of unvoiced fears,
In the silence, we shed our tears.
Each lingering glance, a promise made,
As embers glow, our doubts will fade.

Together we weave a sacred bond,
A shelter built, and love responds.
In the tapestry of silent care,
We find our courage, strong and rare.

Tapestry of Connection

Threads of life intertwine and weave,
In every moment, we believe.
Stitches of laughter, ties of tears,
A tapestry rich with shared years.

In the fabric of time, love is sewn,
Connecting souls, never alone.
Rainbow hues in every strand,
A masterpiece crafted by hand.

With every challenge, we grow strong,
In harmony, we right the wrong.
Embracing differences, side by side,
In this vast world, a joyful ride.

Paths we walk are never straight,
Yet in our bond, we celebrate.
Each knot, a lesson, a cherished gift,
In our connection, hearts uplift.

Together we stitch our hope and dreams,
In this tapestry, love redeems.
A portrait of us, so beautifully spun,
In the art of connection, we are one.

The Essence of Unity

In every heart beats a common song,
Together we rise, where we belong.
Hand in hand, we walk the same path,
Embracing the strength in our shared laugh.

Through trials faced, we stand as one,
In the dance of life, we've only begun.
With courage sewn in each woven thread,
Our hopes intertwine, where love is spread.

From distant shores, our voices blend,
Creating a harmony that knows no end.
In kindness and grace, we build our trust,
Turning to unity, as we must.

With every sunrise, a new chance to see,
The beauty of what we can be.
Together in spirit, we forge a way,
In the essence of unity, where hearts sway.

Tapestry of Tenderness

Threads of kindness, woven tight,
In the fabric of love, we find our light.
With every touch, gentle and warm,
We craft a bond, a protective charm.

Soft whispers float in the evening air,
Carried on breezes, free and rare.
In shared moments, our spirits soar,
In the tapestry of tenderness, we explore.

Each smile a stitch, each laugh a hue,
Painting our world in vibrant view.
Through storms we weather, we hold each other,
In this life journey, there's no other.

Unraveling fears, we find our way,
In the embrace of love, we choose to stay.
With vibrant shades, our hearts expand,
Creating a masterpiece, hand in hand.

In the Embrace of Silence

In quiet moments, love softly speaks,
A tender language that never seeks.
With every sigh, a story unfolds,
In the embrace of silence, our hearts hold.

Beneath the stars, where shadows blend,
Together we find the peace we send.
In stillness shared, our souls unite,
Wrapped in the warmth of a starry night.

Time slows down in this sacred space,
Each heartbeat echoes, a calming grace.
The world outside fades into the night,
In the embrace of silence, we take flight.

Holding hands, we breathe as one,
In the hush of dusk, where dreams are spun.
With whispers fading, all worries cease,
In the embrace of silence, we find peace.

Finding Sanctuary in Each Other

In your eyes, I find my home,
A sanctuary where I can roam.
With every smile, a gentle light,
Guiding me through the darkest night.

In your arms, the world feels right,
A refuge built from love's pure sight.
We share a space where hearts can mend,
Finding sanctuary that will not end.

Through laughter shared, we break down walls,
In this haven, love gently calls.
In every story told, we weave
A tapestry of trust, we believe.

As seasons change and time moves on,
In each other's hearts, we stay strong.
Finding peace in the chaos, together we roam,
In the sanctum of love, we've found our home.

Sculpting Bonds of Trust

In whispers shared, we find our ground,
Each secret kept, a treasure found.
Through shadows thick, we dare to tread,
In every word, our hearts are wed.

With open hands, we sculpt the clay,
Molding dreams in light of day.
Each promise cast, a firm embrace,
In every challenge, we find our grace.

Through trials faced and laughter shared,
In moments quiet, hearts prepared.
We build a space where truth can bloom,
In trust, we find our sacred room.

With every heartbeat, ties unwind,
In silent nods, our paths aligned.
We weave the threads of hope and care,
In bonds of trust, we lay them bare.

Together strong, we'll face the storm,
In unity, our spirits warm.
With every step, we rise anew,
In sculpted bonds, our promise true.

Echoes of Togetherness

In laughter shared, our voices blend,
Through every joy, our hearts extend.
We dance in sync, like waves at sea,
In echoes strong, we find the key.

Together we weave stories bright,
In tender moments, pure delight.
With every glance, our souls ignite,
In shadows cast, we bring the light.

From gentle words, our strength arises,
Navigating life with sweet surprises.
In whispered dreams, our hopes align,
In echoes of love, the stars entwine.

In every shared silence, we understand,
The warmth of connection, a guiding hand.
We rise and fall, yet never part,
In echoes of togetherness, one heart.

With arms embraced, we face the night,
In unity's glow, everything feels right.
Together we'll journey, side by side,
In echoes of love, forever abide.

Building Bridges of Understanding

With open minds, we take our stand,
In every glance, a guiding hand.
Through words we share, we start to see,
In bridges built, we set hearts free.

Each story told, a path we lay,
In kindness found, we find our way.
With every thought, a new perspective,
In understanding, love's directive.

Through laughter, tears, we find our ground,
In simple acts, true bonds are found.
Our differences, a strength we see,
In bridges built, we choose to be.

With courage bright, we face the fray,
In every struggle, our hearts will sway.
Together strong, we reach the shore,
In building bridges, we find much more.

Hand in hand, we walk this line,
In harmony's glow, our spirits shine.
With every bridge, we rise above,
In understanding, we find our love.

The Art of Being Seen

In quiet moments, presence shines,
We see the heart in subtle signs.
Each glance exchanged, a silent chord,
In every breath, our truth restored.

With open hearts, we learn to see,
The beauty in vulnerability.
Through every story, layer unfolds,
In art of being seen, we hold.

In honesty's light, we find our voice,
In every choice, a sacred choice.
With gentle strength, we dare to share,
In openness, we find the rare.

With listening ears, we bridge the gap,
In every word, we close the lap.
Through understanding, souls align,
In art of being seen, we shine.

Together we'll explore the depths,
In every moment, taking breaths.
In shared connection, we rise and glow,
In art of being seen, love grows.

Threads of Intimacy

In whispers soft as morning dew,
We share our secrets, just us two.
Each laugh a stitch, each sigh a seam,
Together we weave our tender dream.

Joy and sorrow in the loom,
Creating warmth that will consume.
A tapestry of moments shared,
With every thread, you know I cared.

In shadows cast, our hearts unite,
Through darkest hours, we find the light.
A comfort found in every glance,
In this embrace, we take our chance.

Each memory spun with golden thread,
In quietude, all words unsaid.
Hand in hand, our journey flows,
An infinite path, where love only grows.

Together we stitch our lives anew,
A vibrant quilt of me and you.
With every touch, our spirits soar,
In threads of intimacy, we explore.

Weaving Hearts Together

Through tangled yarns, our spirits blend,
A masterpiece that will not end.
Each heartbeat syncs a rhythmic tune,
In starry nights beneath the moon.

With every loop, our laughter rings,
A woven fabric of countless things.
In colors bright, we paint our skies,
With every moment, love defies.

Gentle hands with purpose bind,
Two drifting souls, fate intertwined.
A dance of fibers, soft and strong,
In unity, we find our song.

Through sun and storm, we face the test,
Together woven, forever blessed.
Our hearts, a tapestry intertwined,
In every thread, our dreams aligned.

With needles poised, we craft with grace,
A legacy that time won't erase.
Weaving hearts, forever in sync,
In life's embrace, our souls will link.

The Fabric of Connection

In every glance, a story's spun,
A fabric rich as setting sun.
With threads of trust and stitches bright,
We shape our world in morning light.

Each moment stitched, a perfect fit,
With memories shared, we lovingly knit.
In laughter's echo, in silence' space,
We find our harmony, a warm embrace.

Frayed edges mend with gentle care,
In tangled paths, love's woven lair.
We gather strength, in unity's name,
In every tear, there's hope, no shame.

Together we stand, a quilt of dreams,
In every heartbeat, our passion gleams.
Together we rise, together we fall,
In the fabric of connection, we have it all.

As seasons shift, our colors may fade,
But in every thread, a promise made.
With hearts aligned in life's grand design,
The fabric of connection, forever entwined.

Embracing the Invisible

In quiet spaces, love takes flight,
Embracing the invisible light.
An unseen bond with every breath,
A dance of souls that conquers death.

With whispers soft, our hearts collide,
In shadows deep, we shall confide.
In moments shared and silent grace,
We find our refuge, our sacred place.

A touch that lingers, yet not seen,
Embracing what lies in between.
In every heartbeat, we share the space,
An ethereal bond in time and place.

Through storms and calm, we feel the truth,
In youthful dreams and fading youth.
Invisible threads, in trust we find,
In each embrace, our hearts aligned.

So let us weave this endless dream,
In love's embrace, we boldly beam.
Though unseen, our spirits will soar,
Embracing the invisible, forevermore.

Pathways of Mutual Understanding

We walk through paths of silent trust,
Each road a bridge, as words combust.
In shared glances, we find our way,
And hearts align at the break of day.

With every step, we learn and grow,
In gardens where our spirits flow.
The echoes of our laughter ring,
As nature whispers what love can bring.

Through storms and shadows, we will strive,
Each shared moment helps us thrive.
We paint the skies with hopes held high,
A canvas wide, where dreams can fly.

In the embrace of this sacred space,
We weave our tales, a soft embrace.
With roots entwined beneath the ground,
In unity, our strength is found.

Together on this winding road,
With open hearts, we share the load.
In every turn, a chance to see,
The light that binds both you and me.

The Warm Embrace of Together

In summer's glow, we find our peace,
A quiet world where worries cease.
With hands held tight, we walk as one,
Through golden fields, beneath the sun.

The laughter shared, a gentle breeze,
In each other's warmth, our hearts find ease.
A quiet moment, a glance so sweet,
In every heartbeat, love's rhythm beats.

We gather dreams beneath the stars,
Each wish a promise, no matter how far.
With every hug, our fears decrease,
In the warm embrace, we find our peace.

Seasons change, but we remain,
Through sunlit joys and hidden pain.
In storms together, we find our way,
In love's bright light, we'll choose to stay.

With every dawn, new hopes we chase,
In every challenge, a strong embrace.
Through journeys shared and tales retold,
In the warmth of us, our hearts unfold.

Starlit Journeys Side by Side

Beneath the stars, our path is clear,
With every heartbeat, I feel you near.
In whispered dreams, we take our flight,
Two souls as one, in the velvet night.

The moonlight guides our steps so far,
Each twinkling light, a wish, a star.
Hand in hand, we stroll through time,
Every moment feels like a rhyme.

In shadows deep, our laughter glows,
Through every challenge, our courage grows.
With eyes aglow, we chase the dawn,
In the starlit world, we feel reborn.

We gather stories in the dark,
In silent spaces, we leave our mark.
With every journey, love's fire burns,
As together, each new lesson learns.

Side by side, our dreams align,
In the vast expanse, our stars entwine.
Together we rise, forever bound,
In starlit journeys, true love is found.

Cherished Corners of Life

In cozy nooks, where memories dwell,
With every story, our hearts compel.
In laughter shared, and whispers soft,
We cherish moments, our spirits aloft.

Through bustling streets and quiet lanes,
In every joy, we break the chains.
In candid glances, the world stands still,
In cherished corners, time bends to will.

We gather joys in little things,
The simple gifts that laughter brings.
In every hug, in every sigh,
Life's treasures bloom as days go by.

In the embrace of twilight's grace,
We find our home, our sacred space.
In happy chaos, our love aligns,
Among these corners, our heart defines.

Together we weave a tapestry bright,
In every stitch, pure love ignites.
From cherished corners, our futures rise,
In every moment, life's sweet surprise.

Threads of Affection

In the quiet night so deep,
Gentle whispers secrets keep.
Stitches woven, hearts align,
Each thread, a moment divine.

Laughter lingers in the air,
Hands held tight, a tender care.
Colors blend, a vibrant hue,
In every fold, I find you.

Winding paths of soft embrace,
Every smile, a warm trace.
Golden memories we weave,
In this love, we believe.

Through the storms and sunny days,
Together we'll find our ways.
Every knot a promise tight,
In our warmth, we find the light.

As seasons change and time moves on,
Our threads will never be gone.
With every stitch, our story grows,
In threads of love, forever flows.

The Fabric of Us

In every corner of the room,
Lies the fabric of our bloom.
Woven with laughter and care,
Threads of hope floating in air.

Your smile is the brightest hue,
Stitched with dreams both old and new.
Together we dance, we sway,
In this fabric, come what may.

Life's tapestry, rich and bold,
Stories shared, warm and gold.
Fading lines, yet vivid still,
In the fabric, love's sweet thrill.

Every patch tells tales we've spun,
Mended moments all in fun.
Comfort found in every seam,
In the fabric lies our dream.

Embracing frays that time might bring,
Layered love in everything.
Together we emerge anew,
In the fabric, I find you.

Embracing the Heartbeat

In silence, hear our hearts unite,
Pulses echo, soft and light.
Fleeting moments, sweet and bright,
Wrapped in love, the stars ignite.

Every gaze, a silent song,
In your presence, I belong.
Gentle rhythms, odd and rare,
Together, we breathe the air.

Through adventures, hand in hand,
Finding joy in grain and sand.
With each heartbeat, worlds collide,
In your warmth, I take my stride.

Soft whispers in the dark,
Light a glow, a vibrant spark.
Embracing futures filled with grace,
In every heartbeat, I find place.

As the seasons twist and turn,
In each rhythm, love will burn.
Together, we'll dance with fate,
Embracing hearts, never late.

Sculpting Bonds of Kindness

With gentle hands, we carve our way,
Chiseling hope day by day.
In the stone, our dreams emerge,
Sculpting love, a sacred urge.

Each kind word, a chisel's grace,
Forms the lines upon your face.
With every touch, our spirits blend,
In this art, there's no end.

Through the trials, we stand tall,
Building strength, we won't fall.
Every gesture, shape anew,
Kindness flows between us two.

Whispers of courage in each breath,
Sculpting life beyond the depths.
Carved with patience, love's own art,
Bound together, heart to heart.

In this journey, we'll aspire,
Crafting pathways, fueled by fire.
With every bond that time refines,
Sculpting kindness, our love shines.

A Whispered Bond

In silent nights where shadows play,
A whispered bond finds its way.
Two souls entwined, a gentle touch,
In secret corners, we mean so much.

With laughter soft, like summer rain,
We share our joys, we hold the pain.
A fragile thread, yet oh so strong,
In harmony, we both belong.

Through whispered dreams and tender sighs,
We build a world beyond the skies.
In every glance, in every breath,
Our hearts converse, defying death.

So let the stars paint our delight,
A whispered bond ignites the night.
With every heartbeat, take my hand,
Together, we will understand.

Canvas of Empathy

On a canvas vast, our colors blend,
In strokes of kindness, hearts extend.
Each shade a story, a truth laid bare,
In the art of love, we find our care.

The whispers of hope in every hue,
An embrace of feelings, fresh and new.
With tender brushes, we paint the scene,
Creating beauty, where we've been.

In the gallery of our shared fate,
We learn to listen, to appreciate.
Each moment cherished, a brush of grace,
In the frame of life, we find our place.

With empathy's light, we shed despair,
A canvas vibrant, beyond compare.
Together we stand, side by side,
In our masterpiece, love will abide.

Chasing Moments Together

In the dawn's glow, we take our flight,
Chasing moments, hearts alight.
With every step, we weave the day,
In laughter's echo, we find our way.

The twilight whispers, secrets share,
As stars awaken, a silent prayer.
Each fleeting second, a treasure to hold,
In the tapestry of dreams, bold.

Through morning's mist, we run and play,
Capturing memories that never fray.
In every heartbeat, joy rings true,
Chasing moments, just me and you.

As twilight fades and shadows blend,
Hand in hand, we'll never end.
For in the chase, we find our home,
In each other's arms, we freely roam.

Nesting in the Heart's Cradle

In the heart's cradle, we softly rest,
Nurtured by love, feeling blessed.
With gentle whispers, dreams take flight,
In twilight's arms, everything feels right.

We weave our hopes like delicate threads,
In cozy corners, our worries shed.
Nestled closely, side by side,
In this sanctuary, we confide.

The world outside fades away,
In this warm space, here we stay.
With laughter's warmth and tears that flow,
In the heart's cradle, our love will grow.

With every heartbeat, love expands,
In this gentle nest, life understands.
A bond unspoken, yet profoundly felt,
In the heart's cradle, our dreams are dealt.

Stitching Shadows to Light

In the quiet dark, we thread our dreams,
We weave our hopes with golden seams.
Each stitch a whisper, a prayer in the night,
Transforming shadows, bringing forth light.

Fingers dance softly, mapping the stars,
Bridging the space between us, no bars.
With every knot, our stories unite,
Stitching shadows, we chase the bright.

In the tapestry's heart, our fears take flight,
Embracing the warmth of the morning's light.
Together we flourish, our colors ignite,
A masterpiece forged in the depths of the night.

Through threads of laughter and sorrows we weave,
Creating a fabric that we both believe.
With courage abundant, our spirits in flight,
Stitching shadows, we bring forth the light.

Hands Joined in Harmony

In the circle of kin, our fingers entwine,
Hearts beat as one, a rhythm divine.
Together we stand, under sky so bright,
Hands joined in harmony, a beautiful sight.

Through trials we face, we lift one another,
In joy and in sorrow, each calls the other.
With whispers of courage, we rise from the fight,
Hands joined in harmony, holding on tight.

The bond we have built, it cannot be broken,
In silence or laughter, it speaks without token.
Together we flourish, our dreams take flight,
Hands joined in harmony, hearts shining bright.

Through seasons that change, our roots run deep,
Nurtured in kindness, our promises keep.
Embracing the journey, with love as our light,
Hands joined in harmony, in day and in night.

Heartfelt Companionship

In cozy corners where memories blend,
With laughter and stories shared with a friend.
Each moment a treasure, a sparkling delight,
Heartfelt companionship, shining so bright.

Side by side, we share every dream,
A bond that's unbreakable, or so it seems.
In silence we find a comforting light,
Heartfelt companionship, day turning to night.

Through the storms we weather, our spirits align,
In the warmth of our hearts, we endlessly shine.
Together we journey, our paths ever right,
Heartfelt companionship, a guiding light.

As seasons may change, our love will remain,
Rooted in trust, like a shelter from rain.
In this shared embrace, our futures ignite,
Heartfelt companionship, a bond to unite.

Echoing Emotions

In the stillness of night, feelings arise,
Whispers of longing beneath starry skies.
Echoes of laughter, fading from sight,
Resonating softly, like shadows in flight.

Each heartbeat a question, each sigh a reply,
In the depths of our souls, truths never lie.
With courage and grace, we honor the plight,
Echoing emotions, in darkness and light.

As memories linger, reflections collide,
In the dance of our hearts, no secrets can hide.
The rhythm of love, a song taking flight,
Echoing emotions, our spirits unite.

Through laughter and tears, through losses and gains,
The pulse of our bond like soft, gentle rains.
In echoes we find, our souls reunite,
Echoing emotions, forever in sight.

Nurturing the Inner Circle

In whispers soft, we gather near,
With hearts entwined, we cast off fear.
Through laughter shared and tears we catch,
Our bond, a fire, none can snatch.

In shadows deep, we seek the light,
With guiding hands, we hold on tight.
Each moment precious, we embrace,
Together we find our sacred space.

As seasons shift, we weather storms,
In unity, our love transforms.
The roots we plant, they grow and spread,
Nurtured in words that often said.

With every heartbeat, trust we weave,
In our small world, we shall believe.
The inner circle, strong and bright,
A tapestry of purest light.

Through every challenge, side by side,
In joy and sorrow, we've applied.
In nurturing, we find the grace,
A lasting bond, time can't erase.

Mosaic of Shared Moments

Each memory a tile, we lay,
In colors bright, a grand display.
With laughter's echo, we create,
A mosaic rich that celebrates.

Through whispered dreams and stories told,
A narrative in hues of gold.
In simple joys, we stitch and thread,
Moments cherished, never shed.

The laughter's dance, the tears that flow,
In this mosaic, love will grow.
Like pieces fitting, side by side,
A vibrant journey, our hearts' pride.

In sunsets painted with our hues,
The canvas broad, we choose to use.
With every sunrise, fresh and bright,
A shared history warms the night.

Bound by threads of time and grace,
This artwork forms our sacred space.
In every glance, a story found,
A mosaic where love knows no bound.

Chiseling Affection's Stone

With patient hands, we start to carve,
Each tender touch, each word, a star.
Our love, a stone, both hard and true,
In every chip, the heart breaks through.

Through struggles faced and trials won,
Together, we shine just like the sun.
Each moment carved, a piece of time,
An artful dance, a sacred rhyme.

The hammer strikes, the dust it flies,
But in that grit, our spirit lies.
With every shape, the bond we mold,
A masterpiece, as love unfolds.

With chisel bright, we smooth the edges,
In every flaw, our love acknowledges.
A statue strong, yet soft inside,
In chiseling, our hearts abide.

Through years that pass, we work as one,
In love's embrace, we come undone.
With each creation, we engage,
Chiseling affection, page by page.

The Dance of Souls Intertwined

In twilight's glow, two shadows meet,
With whispers soft, they sway and greet.
A dance begins, hearts in align,
Where souls unite, and spirits shine.

Each step a story, lightly tread,
In rhythm found, where fears have fled.
With each embrace, the world goes dim,
The dance of souls, a sacred hymn.

In laughter's lift and sorrow's sway,
Together, we find our own ballet.
Through twirls and spins, we write our song,
In this grand dance, we all belong.

Like leaves that twirl in autumn's breeze,
We find the flow, we find our ease.
Through notes of joy and gentle sighs,
This dance of souls is where love lies.

As music fades and silence reigns,
In stillness deep, our love remains.
With every beat, our spirits twine,
Forever lost in dance, divine.

The Light in Shared Shadows

In quiet corners where we dwell,
A flicker shines, a soft farewell.
Hand in hand, we face the night,
Finding warmth in shared light.

Our laughter dances, free and bold,
In whispered tales that we have told.
Beneath the stars, our spirits soar,
Glimmers of hope forevermore.

Through the darkness, we will roam,
Creating paths that feel like home.
In shadows cast, we find our way,
The light within will always stay.

Though storms may brew, and doubts take flight,
Together still, we reignite.
With every heartbeat, trust we bind,
The light we share, forever kind.

So let us stand, both strong and bold,
In this dance, our love enfold.
In every shadow, find the spark,
Together, lighting up the dark.

Unraveling the Ties That Bind

Each thread a story, woven tight,
In tangled webs of day and night.
As hands entwine, we learn to see,
The bonds that hold, yet set us free.

In moments shared, we find our ground,
Our hearts beat out a sacred sound.
Desires clashed and dreams collide,
In every twist, love will abide.

With whispers soft, we pry apart,
Each silent cause, a broken heart.
To understand the ties we share,
In every tear, a hidden care.

As threads unravel, truth we find,
The past is lost, yet love's not blind.
In every stitch, a chance to mend,
With open hearts, we can transcend.

So let us tread with gentle feet,
Where love's embrace and sorrows meet.
In unraveling, new paths will wind,
Through every tie, a heart aligned.

A Symphony of Heartbeats

In the silence, pulses ignite,
A rhythm soft, a dance of light.
Where every thump transcends the air,
In harmony, we shed our care.

Each moment shared, a note in time,
With every glance, a whispered rhyme.
A melody of souls entwined,
In every beat, our love defined.

Through trials faced, our song remains,
In stormy nights and sunny plains.
Resonating, the echoes call,
A symphony that breaks the fall.

As heartstrings pull, we bend, we sway,
In this embrace, let music play.
Together, we compose the sound,
In every heart, our love is found.

So let the world hear our refrain,
Through every joy, through every pain.
In this grand symphony we cast,
A dance of heartbeats, boundless, vast.

The Portrait of Us

In hues of love, we paint the day,
With every stroke, we find our way.
A canvas born from dreams we share,
In every line, a truth laid bare.

The shadows play, the light will dance,
In vibrant shades, we take our chance.
With deepening colors, stories flow,
A portrait blooms, and hearts will glow.

Each brush of fate, a tender place,
Where laughter lives and time finds grace.
In every glance, a treasure found,
In every whisper, love unbound.

So here we stand with hearts alive,
In this artwork, we will thrive.
Together framed, our souls express,
A masterpiece of happiness.

With every layer, deeper still,
In this portrait, love we fulfill.
A journey shared, forever thus,
In vibrant tones, the portrait of us.

Interwoven Dreams

In the quiet dusk, we start to weave,
Threads of whispers, hopes that believe.
Stars align in a tapestry bright,
Painting our wishes, stitched with light.

Fingers entwined, we gather the night,
A dance of shadows, hearts take flight.
Through the fabric, stories unfold,
Interwoven dreams in strands of gold.

Each sigh a promise, a gentle thread,
Filling the spaces that silence bred.
In every glance, a flicker of fate,
We mold the future, we create.

With every heartbeat, the pattern shifts,
In the loom of time, serenity lifts.
Together we stand, against the storm,
In our woven dreams, we are reborn.

The night may fall, but we still glow,
Each dream we nurture begins to grow.
In the world's fabric, our hearts align,
Interwoven, forever divine.

Ties of Sacred Trust

In the garden where secrets bloom,
We cultivate the space, dispel the gloom.
Hands joined together, we nurture the roots,
With whispers of love, our spirit shoots.

Promises made, like vines entwined,
In the heart's chamber, our souls combined.
Through every trial, our bond holds strong,
In the dance of life, we belong.

Tempests may come, but we will stand,
Each heartbeat echoing, hand in hand.
With trust as our anchor, we'll brave the sea,
A sacred alliance, forever free.

In the shadows, light can still play,
Our ties of trust will never fray.
Together we rise, against the tide,
In the sacred space where hearts abide.

Let the world witness what we've become,
A testament to love, a resonant drum.
In every challenge, in every gust,
We'll prevail, bound by sacred trust.

The Gentle Pull

A subtle tug, a whispered call,
In the still of night, when shadows fall.
Between the stars, our spirits glide,
A cosmic bond that will not hide.

The moon observes our secret dance,
Guiding us softly, a fleeting chance.
With every heartbeat, the pull draws near,
In the vastness, it's you I hear.

Through dreams, we wander, hand in hand,
In the unseen, we make our stand.
An ebbing current, a flowing stream,
Together we chase that silver beam.

The gentle pull, an unbroken thread,
Wherever it leads, we'll never dread.
In the quiet moments, we're intertwined,
In the sacred silence, our souls aligned.

As dawn breaks softly, the shadows wane,
We'll follow the pull, through joy and pain.
In the heart of the universe, still we'll roam,
With every pull, we find our home.

Blooming in Shared Spaces

In the sunlight's glow, we take our stance,
Petals unfurl in a joyful dance.
Together we grow, roots intertwined,
In shared spaces, love is defined.

Each drop of rain, a gentle kiss,
Nurturing dreams, a garden of bliss.
With vibrant colors, we paint our days,
Blooming together in countless ways.

Through storms that pass, we bend but don't break,
In every challenge, new paths we make.
A spectrum of hope, a canvas so wide,
Blooming in spaces where hearts abide.

We celebrate life in the moments we share,
In the fragrance of love, we exhale care.
As the seasons change, our roots grow deep,
In the garden of trust, our dreams we keep.

Forever we flourish, side by side,
In this sacred space, we take our pride.
With boundless beauty, our spirits race,
Together we thrive, blooming in shared spaces.

Unfolding the Layers of Us

Each moment unfolds a piece,
In laughter, in silence, we tease.
Layers of stories, we share,
Building a bond, beyond compare.

In the light, we find our way,
Through shadows that softly play.
Every layer, a tale untold,
In the warmth, together, we're bold.

Gentle whispers of the past,
Embracing the truths that last.
With every look, we uncover,
The essence of one another.

As petals of time reveal,
The beauty that we can feel.
Unraveling threads intertwined,
A tapestry of hearts aligned.

In the dance of life, we sway,
Guided by the dreams we lay.
With every heartbeat, we trust,
Unfolding the layers of us.

The Heart's Compass

In every beat, a path is drawn,
Guided by love's tender dawn.
With every choice, a step we take,
The heart's compass will not break.

It points toward the brightest light,
In moments lost, it brings the sight.
Through trials and fears, we find our way,
With faith, we seek, come what may.

When the world feels cold and gray,
The heart whispers, "Stay, don't stray."
A gentle pull, a nudge so kind,
It leads us back to what we find.

In quiet moments, it sings soft,
With dreams that lift our spirits aloft.
Each heartbeat sings, a song so sweet,
The rhythm of love's flowing beat.

The heart's compass will ever lead,
To places where we plant the seed.
With every turn, it binds us close,
In the journey, it's love we chose.

Quiet Reveries of Connection

In whispered thoughts, we find our peace,
Where time slows down, and worries cease.
Quiet moments shared in still,
Building a bond, a sacred will.

The world fades out, we come alive,
In these reveries, our hearts thrive.
Glimmers of trust, a gentle grace,
In this stillness, we embrace.

As stars align in the night sky,
We weave our dreams, let our spirits fly.
In the hush, our stories blend,
In gentle echoes, love will mend.

The beauty in the simple things,
In laughter and the joy it brings.
A glance, a smile, a knowing heart,
In quiet reveries, we won't part.

Together we dance in the moon's glow,
In the serenity that we both know.
With each heartbeat, a promise made,
In these quiet moments, we are laid.

Whispers of Togetherness

In every glance, a whisper flows,
In soft caresses, love bestows.
Through gentle sighs, we share our dreams,
In harmony, our hearts it seems.

With every word, a promise spun,
In the warmth, we become one.
Together, through trials we move,
In whispers of love, we find our groove.

The world outside may roar and clash,
But in our space, we find a bash.
With laughter's echo and tender touch,
In this togetherness, we feel so much.

As seasons turn, our bond will grow,
In every heartbeat, love will flow.
Through whispered hopes and grace divine,
In togetherness, our fates entwine.

With every moment, we ignite,
A flame that warms, that feels so right.
In whispers soft, we find our way,
Together, forever, come what may.

The Palette of Affection

In hues of red, love's warm embrace,
The gentle touch, a soft trace.
With strokes of blue, calmness flows,
In vibrant greens, our garden grows.

Each color speaks, a silent song,
Binding us where we belong.
In every shade, a story told,
A canvas rich, a heart of gold.

Pastels whisper of tender days,
While bold colors mark our ways.
With every stroke, our love awakes,
In this art, our spirit shakes.

Together we blend, a masterpiece,
In this gallery, our hearts find peace.
As time unfolds, our colors blend,
In the palette of love, we transcend.

With every layer, our bond grows tight,
Painting dreams in the still of night.
In every shade, a lifetime swings,
The palette dances, as our heart sings.

Shadows Dancing in Light

In twilight's glow, shadows play,
Whispered secrets in their ballet.
Soft movements step on tender ground,
As dreams and dusk begin to sound.

They sway and dip with gentle grace,
Each twirl, a transient embrace.
In the glow, they twist and twine,
A fleeting moment, pure and divine.

Against the light, they stretch and fawn,
Chasing dusk, beckoning dawn.
In the shimmer, they start to blur,
Like a silent song, they stir.

Feeling the pulse of night's caress,
Dancing shadows, a mystical mess.
With every flicker, stories spin,
As night unfolds, new beginnings begin.

They vanish softly as day appears,
Leaving whispers in our ears.
In the sunlight, they take their flight,
Shadows dancing in the light.

Brushed by Solitude

In the stillness, time unfolds,
Whispers of thoughts, quietly told.
Among the silence, peace does bloom,
In solitude, I find my room.

Each moment still, a breath to take,
In calm embrace, my heart won't break.
With every sigh, my thoughts collide,
In solitude, I choose to hide.

The world outside may rush and race,
But here it's still, a gentle space.
In quiet corners, echoes rest,
In solitude, I feel the best.

Brush of the wind, echoes near,
Every whisper, I can hear.
In solitude's arms, I softly sway,
Lost in moments, I drift away.

Each day unfolds with tender grace,
Within this space, I find my place.
Brushed by thoughts, I softly blend,
In solitude, my heart can mend.

Harmonious Hearts

In symphony, our hearts collide,
With melodies that coincide.
A dance of notes, a gentle sway,
In harmony, we find our way.

Each rhythm speaks of love's embrace,
In tender whispers, we find grace.
With every beat, a story flows,
In harmonious tides, our spirit glows.

Together we weave a tapestry bright,
An orchestra of day and night.
In the silence, our voices blend,
In this union, hearts transcend.

From highs and lows, we learn and grow,
In sync with life, we ebb and flow.
Each note a promise, strong and true,
In harmony, it's me and you.

The song of us will never fade,
In every chord, love is laid.
In this music of souls, we'll start,
Forever joined, harmonious hearts.

The Invisible Thread

In silence we weave, stories unfold,
A tapestry bright, with threads of gold.
Each moment a stitch, in the fabric we share,
Binding hearts gently, with love in the air.

Through trials we twine, our hopes and our fears,
With whispers of strength, we conquer our tears.
Invisible ties, they lead us along,
A melody sweet, like an ancient song.

In shadows and light, our paths intertwine,
A dance of the souls, your hand in my mine.
In each woven strand, a promise we find,
An echo of trust, in the heart and the mind.

The journey is long, yet we journey as one,
With laughter and warmth, we bask in the sun.
Together we stand, through thick and through thin,
In the fabric of life, our love will begin.

So cherish the thread, though it may be unseen,
For in every weave, is where we've both been.
With gratitude, we stitch, our stories collide,
In the quilt of existence, forever our guide.

When Souls Align

In the quiet of dusk, our spirits ignite,
Two fires converge, in the softening light.
With laughter and tears, we dance through the night,
When souls align, everything feels right.

The universe hums, in a rhythm divine,
Echoes of truth, as our lives intertwine.
In glimpses of grace, we discover our way,
Together we rise, come what may.

With whispered confessions, the barriers fall,
In the space between, we surrender it all.
Like stars in the sky, we brighten the dark,
When souls align, we leave our mark.

Through storms that may rage, we weather as one,
With faith as our anchor, we'll never be done.
In the depths of our hearts, a radiant shine,
A symphony sweet, when our souls align.

In moments so fleeting, we find our own peace,
An eternal embrace, where doubts all cease.
When the world fades away, it's just you and I,
Holding tightly together, as minutes go by.

Threads of Serenity

In a world full of chaos, we find our flow,
Stitching together the love that we know.
With gentle intentions, we weave and we spin,
Creating a haven, where calm can begin.

With each tender knot, we tether our dreams,
In the quiet of heart, tranquility beams.
The fabric of peace, through every embrace,
Threads of serenity, a warm, soft place.

Through trials and storms, we bolster our care,
Building a refuge, we choose to share.
In the silence we gather, the world brushed away,
We nurture our hearts, come what may.

Like rivers that blend, our souls intertwine,
Flowing together, in rhythm and rhyme.
With trust as our guide, and love as our aim,
Threads of serenity, remain the same.

In the fabric of life, we sew our delight,
With colors of joy, we banish the night.
Creating a sanctuary, one thread at a time,
In this tapestry bright, our spirits will climb.

Nurturing the Embrace

In the warmth of your arms, a universe blooms,
A sanctuary soft, where love gently looms.
With whispers of comfort, the chaos subsides,
Nurturing the embrace, where true love abides.

In the dance of the hearts, with each sacred beat,
We forge a connection, both tender and sweet.
Through laughter and tears, like seasons we change,
With roots deeply planted, our bond feels so strange.

With flourishes bold, we cultivate trust,
In the garden of life, it's the must of the must.
As petals unfold, in the cool morning dew,
Nurturing the embrace, with each moment new.

With every soft touch, and each whispered plea,
We sow understanding, in love's gentle sea.
As shadows retreat, and the sun lingers long,
In nurturing the embrace, we find where we belong.

Through challenges faced, our spirits will blend,
With each step we take, hand in hand till the end.
In unity's glow, we eternally shine,
Nurturing the embrace, forever divine.

Soft Threads of Encouragement

In shadows long, a light will gleam,
A whisper soft, a gentle dream.
Each word a stitch, a woven guide,
To lift the heart, our hopes collide.

A canvas bright, painted with care,
In every thread, love's truth laid bare.
Embrace the warmth, the bonds we share,
Together we rise, beyond despair.

With every tear, a strength will flow,
In times of doubt, let courage grow.
A tapestry of joy and pain,
Remind us all, we're not in vain.

So hold my hand, through thick and thin,
In this vast world, we both shall win.
For every struggle, there's a chance,
To bloom anew, in life's grand dance.

Through seasons change, with hearts aligned,
Soft threads of hope, our lives entwined.
A quilt of dreams, a steadfast shield,
With love's embrace, we shall not yield.

The Dance of Duality

In light and dark, we find our way,
The sun will rise, the night will sway.
With every step, the balance sings,
A rhythm shared, as life unfolds its wings.

In laughter sweet, in sorrow's grip,
We learn to sail, we learn to slip.
Two sides of life, they intertwine,
A dance of shadows, a waltz divine.

From chaos born, to silence found,
In every heartbeat, we are bound.
The waltz of joy, the sway of pain,
In every pulse, our truth remains.

With open hearts, we take this chance,
To navigate the cosmic dance.
Embrace the light, accept the night,
In duality, we find our might.

For every dawn, the dusk appears,
In every smile, in every tear.
The dance goes on, an endless flow,
In unity, we come to know.

Caressing the Bonds

In every touch, a story told,
With tender grace, the heart unfolds.
A silent vow, a warm embrace,
Together we journey, a sacred space.

Through trials faced, we find our way,
In every moment, come what may.
Like rivers merge, so do our souls,
In love's warm arms, we find our roles.

With whispered words, we weave the ties,
Like stars that glow in endless skies.
Each bond we build, a steadfast chain,
To face the storms, to dance in rain.

In laughter shared, in sorrows deep,
The promises made, our hearts will keep.
With time as thread, our lives entwined,
In every breath, affection kind.

So let us cherish, the bonds we weave,
In gentle knowing, we believe.
For in this world, where dreams expand,
Together we rise, hand in hand.

Heartbeats in Sync

With every beat, a rhythm flows,
Two hearts united, and love knows.
In silent moments, our spirits dance,
In harmony's embrace, we take a chance.

Through every trial, our pulse remains,
In stormy weather, within the strains.
Connected deep, like roots beneath,
In breaths exchanged, we find our myth.

With laughter bright, and tears that gleam,
Our heartbeats echo, a shared dream.
A symphony played, with notes so rare,
In unity found, we breathe the air.

Together we stand, against the tide,
Our hopes ignited, forever tied.
In whispers soft, through struggles vast,
With every moment, a love to last.

So here we dwell, in this sweet song,
With heartbeats in sync, we both belong.
In the tapestry of time, we blend,
With every beat, our story penned.

Beneath the Surface

In shadows deep, secrets lie,
Whispers of dreams, a silent sigh.
Roots intertwine, beneath the ground,
The pulse of life, a tranquil sound.

Ripples dance on the still water,
Echoes of past, a gentle slaughter.
Fish dart swiftly, unseen by most,
Beneath the waves, they play and boast.

Tides unfurl with the moon's embrace,
A secret world, a hidden place.
Currents hold stories untold,
In depths of blue, adventures bold.

Each bubble rises, a fleeting thought,
Threads of connection, love is sought.
Beneath the surface, we are awake,
Unraveling mysteries, ours to make.

Where light and shadow intertwine,
Life's hidden gems, pure and divine.
In the quiet, we find our peace,
Beneath the surface, all fears cease.

We Merge

Two rivers flow, in gentle grace,
Winding together, a shared space.
Currents meet, in harmonized blend,
A journey shared, a path we fend.

Through the valleys, we drift and sway,
Hand in hand, we find our way.
In the echoes of laughter past,
Moments cherished, forever cast.

Hearts align, like stars above,
Guided by the light of love.
In the tapestry of life we weave,
United souls, we dare believe.

With every step, we strengthen our bond,
In the quiet, we respond.
Each heartbeat sings a timeless song,
Together forever, where we belong.

Merging dreams, forever entwined,
One rhythm beats, one love defined.
As we flow, let worries fade,
In this union, our fears betrayed.

The Quilt of Familiarity

Stitched with care, memories sewn,
Each patch a story, a journey known.
Patterns of laughter, tears alike,
Woven together, a shared hike.

Every thread holds tales of old,
A tapestry bright, a warmth to behold.
Colors vibrant, faded hue,
The quilt embraces me and you.

Familiar comforts, a gentle touch,
In quiet moments, we feel so much.
Wrapped in warmth, our hearts collide,
In this embrace, we do not hide.

Through storms and suns, the quilt remains,
Echoes of joy, the soothing pains.
Holding us close, in times of need,
A patchwork of love, a sacred deed.

As seasons change, the quilt will grow,
With memories new, and love's gentle flow.
In familiarity's arms, we find our place,
A quilt of life, our sacred space.

Harmonizing Our Frequencies

Two voices blend, a perfect tune,
Under the glow of a silver moon.
Melodies dance in the night air,
Intertwined rhythms, sweet and rare.

With every note, our souls align,
In the symphony, you are mine.
Resonance deepens, a timeless bond,
Harmonizing hearts, of which we're fond.

Echoes of laughter, whispers of dreams,
Waves of connection, like flowing streams.
In the music, we find our way,
A journey of joy, come what may.

As the starlight wraps us tight,
In this harmony, we take flight.
Each beat a story, each chord a kiss,
In our frequencies, we find bliss.

Together we sing, our voices soar,
In the rhythm of love, we explore.
Harmonizing dreams, we make it real,
In the symphony of hearts, we heal.

Unspoken Rituals of Bonding

In silence shared, a knowing glance,
Quiet laughter, a sacred dance.
Hands entwined, without a word,
In unspoken bonds, love is stirred.

Morning light spills on our skin,
Rituals of comfort, deep within.
A touch that speaks, a gentle sigh,
In these soft moments, we learn to fly.

Shared cups of tea, glances that last,
Fragrant memories of the past.
In the mundane, we find the gold,
In unspoken rituals, a story told.

An unturned page, a silent space,
In your presence, I find my place.
With every heartbeat, we understand,
In the silence, we take a stand.

Through storms we weather, side by side,
In sacred trust, we confide.
Together we forge, without a sound,
Unspoken rituals forever bound.

The Sanctuary of Shared Dreams

In whispers soft, we weave our tales,
Beneath the stars, where hope prevails.
With eyes aglow, we chart our skies,
In this sanctuary, our spirits rise.

Together we paint, with colors bright,
Each stroke a vow, a bond of light.
In laughter's echo, we find our way,
In this sacred space, forever stay.

As shadows dance, our fears take flight,
Within this realm, all wrongs feel right.
We dream of worlds, yet to be found,
In the heartbeat of love, we are unbound.

Through storms we walk, united as one,
In darkest nights, we greet the sun.
With every heartbeat, our journey sings,
In the sanctuary, we are kings.

And when the dawn begins to break,
We gather joy for future's sake.
In shared dreams deep, our paths align,
In this haven, forever shine.

Beyond the Horizon of Solitude

In silence deep, where oceans sigh,
Loneliness fades, dreams learn to fly.
Beyond the horizon, a light shines clear,
A call to venture, casting out fear.

With every step on this winding shore,
Hope awakens, we long for more.
Each wave a reminder, we've come so far,
Together we chase, our guiding star.

Through peaks and valleys, we boldly tread,
Collecting moments, like seeds we've spread.
In whispered winds, our stories blend,
Beyond the horizon, love has no end.

As clouds dissolve and skies grow bright,
We find our home in shared delight.
In unity's cradle, shadows retreat,
Together we rise, strong on our feet.

So let the journey stretch far and near,
With hearts aflame, we conquer our fear.
Beyond the horizon, a promise remains,
In the dance of life, love forever reigns.

The Palette of Our Togetherness

With hues of laughter, we start to blend,
Creating a canvas, where colors transcend.
Each stroke a memory, vivid and bright,
In the palette we craft, we find our light.

From quiet whispers to joyous shouts,
Every shade tells what love's about.
In splashes of kindness, we find our way,
In this artwork of life, we choose to stay.

Amidst the chaos, we find our peace,
In shared creations, our joys increase.
With every heartbeat, a stroke anew,
The masterpiece grows, just me and you.

Through shadows and sunlight, our brush will glide,
In the palette of dreams, we take in stride.
With every color, our souls intertwine,
In this dance of togetherness, love will shine.

So let us paint through each passing day,
With vibrant moments that never decay.
In the palette of life, forever we'll be,
Two hearts, one canvas, in harmony.

Footprints in the Sand of Time

As tides retreat, our footprints show,
A journey shared, where memories flow.
Each step we take along the shore,
In grains of time, we leave much more.

With laughter echoing, waves proclaim,
The sweetest moments, in love's name.
Beneath the sun, we wander free,
In every print, a story to see.

Though waves may wash the past away,
In our hearts, those moments stay.
With every tide, new paths emerge,
In the dance of life, we boldly surge.

Through storms we stand, hand in hand,
Our footprints bold on shifting sand.
A testament to love, steadfast and true,
In the sands of time, I walk with you.

So let us cherish, every trace,
In the tapestry of time and space.
Together we write, with love's own design,
Footprints forever, intertwined.

The Garden of Mutual Growth

In soil rich and dark, we plant our seeds,
With care and trust, we tend to each need.
Side by side, we water dreams anew,
A garden blooms, made up of me and you.

The sun shines bright, our hearts intertwine,
With every moment, our roots align.
Through gentle rains, we learn to bend,
Together we thrive, a love without end.

Each flower blossoms, colors intertwined,
In this sacred space, our souls unwind.
We nurture joy, we gather from pain,
In the garden of growth, love will remain.

Seasons may change, yet we hold on tight,
Through storms and struggles, we find our light.
For in this soil, where our dreams take flight,
The garden of us is forever bright.

Hand in hand, we cultivate the days,
With laughter and tears, in myriad ways.
A sanctuary built from heartbeats and vows,
In the garden of love, we stand as we plough.

Collages of Love

In fragments scattered, we start to create,
Each memory shared, a piece of our fate.
Photos and whispers, laughter and sighs,
A collage of moments, where true love lies.

With colors of passion, we paint our path,
Composing a future, escaping the wrath.
Every touch whispers, every glance beams,
In this artful life, we live out our dreams.

Textures of warmth woven with care,
Every heartbeat echoes, a love we can share.
We piece together the bits and the parts,
Crafting a story that dances in hearts.

Through hues of adventure, we find our voice,
In shades of uncertainty, we make our choice.
Each fragment a treasure, a tale that we tell,
In the collage of love, we weave our spell.

So here's to the canvas, our lives intertwined,
A masterpiece crafted, where souls are aligned.
In the gallery of time, let our love shine through,
For in these collages, our hearts will renew.

Heartstrings in Unison

In quiet moments, our heartstrings align,
With gentle whispers, your heart calls to mine.
Each beat a reminder, a dance in the air,
In the symphony of love, we both find our share.

Through peaks and valleys, the music plays on,
A melody cherished, a bond that won't be gone.
With rhythm unbroken, we sway to the song,
In this tapestry woven, we both belong.

Together we sing, with voices so clear,
In harmony wrapped, we conquer all fear.
With every note lifted, our spirits arise,
A chorus of love, beneath endless skies.

Creating a anthem, our hearts beat as one,
Lit by the magic, of moon and sun.
With love's sweet refrain, we find our own way,
In the symphony of moments, forever we'll stay.

So let the music play, let the echoes flow,
In the symphony of us, together we grow.
For every heartstring, a thread in the night,
In the music of love, we eternally write.

A Kaleidoscope of Affection

In every glance, a swirl of bright hues,
A glimpse of the beauty, in all that we choose.
Colors collide, creating delight,
In this kaleidoscope, our love shines so bright.

Through laughter and joy, we capture the bliss,
In moments so fleeting, we find our true kiss.
Each turn reveals, a spectrum anew,
In this dance of affection, just me and you.

The world spins around, with patterns so grand,
Each twist and each turn, we soar hand in hand.
With tender reflections, we cherish the view,
In the kaleidoscope's magic, our love feels so true.

With shades of compassion, and strokes of care,
We paint our emotions, a canvas to share.
Each fragment a wonder, each piece holds a spark,
In the kaleidoscope's heart, we'll light up the dark.

So let's spin together, forever entwined,
In this vibrant adventure, our souls intertwined.
For in this embrace, our colors will dance,
In the kaleidoscope of love, we find our romance.

The Alchemy of Together

In the quiet of shared dreams,
We forge our hopes in whispered seams.
Two hearts united, the spark ignites,
Transforming shadows into radiant lights.

Each laugh, a gem in the treasure chest,
Every tear shared, a soothing rest.
We blend our colors in vibrant shades,
In togetherness, true magic cascades.

Through trials faced, our bond will grow,
In storms we weather, love's fire will glow.
We are the alchemists of our fate,
Crafting joy as we cultivate.

In moments fleeting, we find our ground,
A tapestry woven, together bound.
With hands entwined, we write our tale,
In the dance of life, we will prevail.

Through every chapter, our echoes ring,
In the symphony of life, we sing.
Together we rise, when shadows descend,
In the alchemy of love, we transcend.

Threads in the Weave of Life

Life's fabric is spun with delicate threads,
Each moment a stitch, where hope gently spreads.
Every encounter, a knot tightly bound,
In the weave of existence, our stories are found.

Colors of laughter, deep hues of sorrow,
Interlace our days, shaping tomorrow.
The golden strand of friendship shines bright,
In the tapestry's glow, we find our light.

With each passing season, we gather and part,
The weave evolves, a work of the heart.
Through trials and triumphs, our patterns align,
In the threads of our lives, design divine.

The weaver's hand guides us through the unknown,
In the shared fabric, we are never alone.
Every thread matters, entwined with care,
In the weave of life, our souls are laid bare.

As the fabric stretches and ages with grace,
We honor each thread, every line, every space.
Together we weave our intricate art,
In the loom of existence, we play our part.

Bridges Over Turbulent Waters

Across the raging rivers we tread,
On bridges of trust, our spirits are led.
Through storms that threaten to pull us apart,
We stand together, with courage of heart.

Each step we take, the foundation is laid,
Through shadows and doubt, our path is displayed.
With hands clasped tight, we traverse the sprawl,
In every challenge, we rise, never fall.

Built from our dreams and whispers of hope,
In turbulent times, we learn how to cope.
The arches we form withstand the fierce tides,
In unity's grip, our strength abides.

The winds may howl, but we will not waver,
Together we chart our course, a favor.
Through the unknown, love's compass will steer,
Over the waters, we conquer our fear.

So let the rivers rage and the waves roar,
On bridges of faith, we'll always explore.
Together we'll rise and claim the day,
With love as our guide, we'll find our way.

Mapping Our Inner Landscapes

In the quiet corners of our minds,
We chart the vistas that love unwinds.
Through valleys of doubt and mountains of grace,
We navigate feelings, each sacred space.

With each breath taken, a path becomes clear,
In the depths of our souls, we hold what's dear.
The rivers of memory, flowing and wide,
Guide us through shadows, with hope as our guide.

We sketch our borders with gentle intent,
Mapping the moments our hearts have lent.
With colors of laughter and shades of our tears,
We honor the journey of all our years.

In the landscape we build, connection is found,
As we traverse the hills, love's pulse resounds.
With each step we take, we honor the past,
Mapping a future where joy can last.

Through storms and sun, we wander with care,
In the map of our lives, each soul laid bare.
Together we journey, side by side we navigate,
In the vastness of being, we celebrate fate.

The Warmth of Presence

In quiet moments, we reside,
The pulse of life, heartbeats collide.
A gentle gaze that holds the light,
In shadowed corners, warmth ignites.

With whispered words, we build our space,
Each laugh, each sigh, a soft embrace.
Together forged, our spirits lift,
In presence found, we share the gift.

Through trials faced, hands intertwined,
In shared resolve, our paths aligned.
We gather strength from all we share,
The warmth of love, beyond compare.

A shelter formed from tender trust,
In every storm, we rise, we must.
With every tear, we learn to grow,
In presence felt, we come to know.

Eclipses fade, yet still we shine,
In fleeting seconds, hands divine.
Through every dawn that breaks anew,
The warmth of presence, me and you.

Interlaced Journeys

Two paths converge in twilight's grace,
Winding stories, time can't erase.
Each step we take, a thread is spun,
Interlaced journeys, hearts as one.

With every turn, the maps unfold,
A tapestry of dreams retold.
Together braving hills and streams,
In whispered hopes, we chase our dreams.

Through winding roads, our laughter flows,
In silent moments, true love grows.
From dusk till dawn, our spirits soar,
Interlaced paths forevermore.

In twilight hours, secrets unfold,
A bond that's forged through tales of old.
With shared horizons, we embark,
Lighting up the midnight dark.

As seasons change, our souls entwine,
In every trial, your hand in mine.
Together still, we find our way,
Interlaced journeys, day by day.

Serenade of Shared Stories

Underneath the starlit skies,
We gather close, where friendship lies.
Each tale we share, a melody,
In harmony, our spirits free.

With every laughter, echoes rise,
A serenade beneath the skies.
The night unfolds with whispers sweet,
In every memory, hearts entreat.

From distant shores to familiar nooks,
We weave the fabric of shared books.
With words that dance, the stories flow,
A tapestry of hearts aglow.

In fireside warmth, our dreams align,
In every glance, our hearts entwine.
With every story told anew,
A serenade that binds us true.

Through timelines crossed and lives embraced,
Together we have found our place.
In moments shared, we craft our tales,
Serenade of stories that never fails.

Roots Beneath the Surface

In whispered winds, the secrets lie,
Roots beneath, where shadows pry.
The earth remembers what we sow,
In silent strength, the stories grow.

A sturdy trunk, where dreams take flight,
In ancient grounds, we seek the light.
Branches reaching toward the sky,
From faithful roots, we learn to fly.

Through seasons change, we bend and sway,
Yet deep below, there's hope to stay.
In twisted trails, our past resides,
Roots beneath, where truth abides.

With every storm, our power shows,
In unity, our spirit glows.
Through fertile soil, our stories run,
Roots intertwined, we are as one.

As time unfolds, the layers peel,
Unveiling hearts that always heal.
Together firm, in love we thrive,
Roots beneath, the soul's alive.

Ties that Bind Gently

In the quiet hours of night,
Whispers ripple soft and light,
Hands entwine, the world fades,
In this bond, our love wades.

Through laughter shared, we grow,
Roots entwined beneath the snow,
When the storms come, we stand strong,
In each other, we belong.

Gentle words like summer rain,
Wash away the hurt and pain,
With every smile, we ignite,
A spark in the darkest night.

In simple moments, love is found,
In echoes of our laughter's sound,
Together through thick and thin,
In our hearts, the warmth within.

So let us cherish every day,
In this dance, we'll find our way,
For in the bonds we've made so true,
I am me, and you are you.

Heartstrings Entwined

Beneath the stars, our dreams take flight,
Two souls woven in the night,
Every glance, a tale untold,
In your warmth, I find my hold.

With every heartbeat, soft and clear,
Your laughter lingers, ever near,
In silence shared, a world unfolds,
A symphony in whispers bold.

Through the valleys deep we roam,
In your arms, I find my home,
Moments cherished, tender grace,
Together, we create our space.

Heartstrings pulled by unseen hands,
Guiding where our spirit stands,
In love's embrace, we rise and fall,
A timeless dance, we heed the call.

So let us weave our story bright,
With colors painted in pure light,
In every sigh, in every glance,
Together, we shall take this chance.

The Dance of Understanding

In gentle steps, we learn to sway,
In rhythm found, we find our way,
With open hearts, we start to see,
The beauty in you, the truth in me.

Every misstep leads us near,
To deeper thoughts we hold so dear,
With eyes that listen, words that flow,
In this dance, our spirits grow.

Together weaving, strong and free,
An understanding tapestry,
Through every twist, we hold on tight,
In shadows cast, we find our light.

With patience wrapped in tender care,
We navigate the depths we share,
In each embrace, we break the mold,
In silence, tales of love are told.

Let's cherish every step, each turn,
In the flame of trust, we brightly burn,
For in this waltz, our souls align,
In harmony, our hearts entwine.

Building Bridges of Trust

With every word, we lay a stone,
In the pathway that we've grown,
Hand in hand, we sculpt our way,
Together facing each new day.

Through trials faced and shadows cast,
Our bond grows stronger, built to last,
In honesty, we find our ground,
In silence shared, our hopes are found.

With laughter bright, we pave the road,
With kindness met, we share the load,
Each moment stitched into the seam,
In trust, we weave our greatest dream.

A bridge across the river wide,
With pillars strong, we'll never hide,
With open arms and hearts aligned,
In unity, our fears behind.

So let us build, with love as guide,
A sanctuary, deep inside,
For every heartbeat, every glance,
In this trust, we find our chance.

Softening Boundaries

Gentle whispers touch the air,
Sailing dreams on currents rare.
Hearts like rivers find their flow,
In the light of souls aglow.

Silent echoes call our names,
In the tapestry, we are flames.
Bridges built with tender grace,
In this realm, we share a space.

Stars align to guide our way,
Uniting night with breaking day.
Each step forward, hands entwined,
In the dance of humankind.

Together we shall rise and soar,
Opening wide a welcoming door.
With each heartbeat, we embrace,
Softening borders, leaving trace.

In this garden, love will bloom,
Casting out all shades of gloom.
Bonds transcending time and place,
A gentle touch, a warm embrace.

Poetic Interludes of Unity

In every line, a story spun,
Harmony dances, two become one.
Words weave melodies so bright,
Uniting hearts in shared delight.

In a world where rhythms blend,
Paths entwine as voices mend.
Verses soar like birds in flight,
In the glow of peaceful light.

Pages turned with hope anew,
Each stanza speaks, ringing true.
In the silence, sweet refrain,
Whispers echo, love's domain.

Bring your dreams, we'll share our fears,
Sounding depths of hidden tears.
In this moment, side by side,
Let our spirits be our guide.

Together through the ebb and flow,
In poetic streams, our passions show.
With every heartbeat, we ignite,
A symphony of shared insight.

A Symphony of Souls

Every heartbeat like a drum,
A melody of what's to come.
Notes of kindness fill the air,
In this symphony, we share.

Strings entwined with love's embrace,
Creating harmonies in space.
Underneath the moonlit sky,
We sing softly, you and I.

From the depths, our voices rise,
As the stars light up the skies.
In this concert of our dreams,
Unity flows like silver streams.

Every whisper holds a tune,
In the dance beneath the moon.
Together, we will compose,
A symphony that gently grows.

In the quiet, our hearts blend,
Beating strong, a heartfelt mend.
With each note, we stand as one,
In this journey, love's begun.

Clusters of Kindred Spirits

Like stars that gather in the night,
We unite, a wondrous sight.
Clusters glowing, sparks in space,
Kindred souls in warm embrace.

From different paths, we have roamed,
In this circle, we find home.
With laughter shared and stories told,
Hearts unfold like petals bold.

Together, weaving tales of old,
Fragments shining, treasures gold.
In the tapestry, we're entwined,
Constellations of humankind.

Let's nurture love, let kindness flow,
In this garden, watch us grow.
A universe of heart and mind,
Clusters of spirits, intertwined.

Through every storm and gentle breeze,
We find comfort, hearts at ease.
In this dance of light, we sway,
Kindred spirits, come what may.

A Tapestry of Affection

Threads of love weave through the night,
Soft whispers glow under the moonlight.
Moments of laughter, shared hands entwined,
In this warm tapestry, our hearts aligned.

Gentle stitches hold memories tight,
Colorful patches, a beautiful sight.
The fabric of trust, so rich and profound,
In every embrace, our solace is found.

Patterns of joy filled with soft grace,
Each gentle touch, a warm, safe place.
Together we craft, with each day anew,
A tapestry bright, forever in view.

Through trials and tears, we stand side by side,
In this woven dream, let love be our guide.
With threads intertwined, we face what may come,
For together in harmony, we are always home.

As seasons will change, so will our hue,
Yet the heart knows a bond that feels true.
In the fabric of life, love's essence will stay,
A tapestry of affection will never fray.

The Invisible Embrace

In shadows we linger, where silence speaks,
A bond unbroken, no words are weak.
The warmth of your presence, a gentle caress,
Invisible embraces, we find our rest.

Through soft glances shared, hearts interlace,
No need for the noise, just feel the space.
A world that fades, yet we're never alone,
In the hush of the night, our love has grown.

In every heartbeat, a whisper of bliss,
Moments unspoken, in love's sweetest kiss.
We wander together, two souls intertwined,
In the invisible, our true hearts aligned.

The air holds our stories, the stars our dreams,
In the quiet connection, nothing is as it seems.
With each breath I take, your essence I find,
In this invisible embrace, our souls are combined.

So let the world turn, with its loud, fray,
We'll find in the silence, a soft, sacred way.
For love needs no language to deeply convey,
The invisible warmth that will never decay.

Nestled in Warmth

Cocooned in the glow of the fireplace light,
We share whispered dreams through the long, cozy night.

Wrapped in blankets, the world fades away,
Nestled in warmth, where our hearts dance and play.

The soft crackle of embers, a rhythm divine,
Your laughter a melody, sweet and benign.
In this little corner, we hold each other near,
Nestled in warmth, our worries disappear.

With cocoa in hand, and the world at bay,
Every moment we cherish, come what may.
In the gentle embrace, life's burdens feel light,
Nestled in warmth, everything feels right.

The quiet of evening, the starlit skies,
In your tender gaze, the universe lies.
With arms all around, love's softest decree,
Nestled in warmth, just you and me.

As the night wears on, let time stand still,
Forever I'll treasure this heart's quiet thrill.
In our sanctuary, hearts perfectly charm,
Nestled in warmth, forever in your arms.

The Circle of Togetherness

In the circle of life, we gather as one,
Through laughter and tears, in the warmth of the sun.
United we stand, hand in hand, hearts free,
In the circle of togetherness, just you and me.

Stories unfold under the celestial dome,
With each voice that echoes, we find our own home.
In moments of stillness, our spirits will soar,
In the circle of togetherness, we are never poor.

From dawn's gentle light to dusk's tender hue,
Each footstep we take, it's me and it's you.
In laughter, in sorrow, we cherish the flow,
In the circle of togetherness, love continues to grow.

Through seasons of change and the storms that we face,
Together, we navigate, filled with grace.
In the rhythm of hearts, our journey we trace,
In the circle of togetherness, we find our place.

So let's hold each other, let the world spin around,
In this sacred circle, our joys will resound.
For as we walk forward, hand in hand we agree,
In the circle of togetherness, we are truly free.